URBAN SPACES

DAVID
KENNETH
SPECTER

PHOTOGRAPHS
BY THE
AUTHOR

International Standard Book Number 0–8212–0463–7
Library of Congress Catalog Card Number 72–93858

First published 1974 by New York Graphic Society Ltd.
140 Greenwich Avenue, Greenwich, Conn. 06830

Designed by Denison Cash Stockman

To Matthew and Evan,
and the cities they will live in

Acknowledgments

I should like to express my thanks to:

The Architectural League of New York, under whose
Arnold W. Brunner Fellowship most of these photographs
were taken.

The Editors of Architectural Record, who first published
some of this material in January 1969, under the title "Some
Essentials of Successful Urban Space."

Forrest Selvig, who originally brought this study to
the attention of the New York Graphic Society.

Denison Cash Stockman, a gifted graphic designer,
for a gratifying collaboration.

D.K.S.

CONTENTS

FOREWORD
BY WALTER MCQUADE

It is late February in New York City. After a deceptively mild December and January the squalid urban winter has taken over: rancid slush, chilling gales, bleakness everywhere. Tenants hunt landlords to plead and protest for more heat. Stoic laborers grunt in a dank hole in the street a few blocks away, repairing an immense water main which blew like a decrepit artery yesterday and spilled five million gallons of ice water into Times Square. The city is turned inward, bearable if experienced as a hive of rooms, but unthinkable as a place for pleasant walking—about as reasonable for living as the wintry North Atlantic is for sailboating. It seems almost not a city, but a condition.

However reluctantly, it must be admitted that the large old American cities are somewhat hostile to humanity, and not only during these depressing months—the grim Februaries and sweltering Augusts. All year round, too many of them suffer from poverty, and also from avarice, as places to be. Granted the city is exciting, but then so is war. The large American industrial-commercial city may, at that, have a certain similarity in tone to war, or, at least, to siege: an interesting patrol here, a tense battle there, but mostly boredom, a waste or limitation of life time. Traffic fuses on city expressways as it does up near a military front during advances and retreats. During rush hours the subways and other tracked transportation recall the general deterioration in traveling conditions across the continent during wartime. There used to be a saying, "Don't you know there's a war on?" to excuse for-the-duration stringencies. Perhaps today we should ask each other, in times of power blackout, transit and garbage pileup, "unacceptable" air, and frustrating crowding, "Don't you know there's a city on?"

This may strike you as a somewhat severe foreword to the volume you have in your hands, a picture book about the environmental pleasures possible in cities; take it as an indication that Mr. Specter's work is seriously purposeful, not just a photographic romp. Seriousness is merited; again, despite a seeming revival of interest in the "quality of living," American cities, particularly the old big ones, are not by and large becoming better places to spend time. It is worth pointing out to U.S. readers that only about a tenth of the illustrations of urban amenities categorized so clearly in this book can be found in their—and the author's—country. Most of them are in Europe.

Why is this? Are our cities too commercial to be gracious places? Must we go back to the souvenir cities of royalty to enjoy unbusinesslike urbanity—waterplay, squares and arcades, glimpses of history preserved, cafés open to promenades, visual surprises and contrived delights of many profitless kinds? It is true that the price of most of these amenities, in human striving and, sometimes, suffering, was paid long ago, and that the imperial will could be ruthless. When Napoleon III agreed to let Baron Haussmann install his famous boulevards in Paris, great anguish ensued because the avenues were run through jammed neighborhoods of the poor (arousing resentment which historians believe had much to do with the Commune of 1871). But urban beauty can be businesslike. Venice, that epitome of charm, was created by very hardheaded traders and warriors. How many fleets of ships could have been built with the investment that went into St. Mark's Square? Instead, some of the Venetians' gold was put into a civic—and religious—expression of their survival and success. It was a *spirited* investment. Maybe that is the quality that has been lacking in most investments in American cities in these years when we have been building as never before.

Perhaps, however, that essential element for good civic construction, the pride of pleasure, is returning. It just may be. Speak carefully, lest it skitter away. Some smart politicians are aware of it in various cities, I think, as well as a whole generation of young architects, and David Specter is one of them. I first met Specter about a year ago, when I was serving on the City Planning Commission of New York, having graciously been appointed by the mayor to be, as he ferociously said, "an enlightened, independent arbiter of taste. . . ." This mayor, John V. Lindsay, recognized urban design as a very worthy rock to polish, but he did more than that; he added staff, and supported new enabling ordinances. A group of young architects was lured to work for the city, equivalent to the young assistant district attorneys who give a few years to the D.A.'s office. These architects were assigned to be the prosecutors, the stalkers of urban graciousness for the City Planning Commission. They began to invent zoning rules which, given the force of law by the Commission, would encourage developers to spend their money on the kinds of environmental improvements which this book treats.

It was not easy, although the basic method was apparent. The city has the power to clamp a lid on the amount of rentable space to be built on any specific site. This limitation inhibits the developer's profit potential. If the city lifts the lid a little, it transpires that the developer becomes willing to pay for some extra amenities at ground level to make up for the extra space upstairs—indeed, he is sometimes willing to reshape the entire building.

Just how the compromise is arrived at depends on the sagacity of both the developer and the city agencies with which he deals. Demanded is honesty and imagination (the latter, at least, not famous as an attribute of either city agencies or developers) and also design talent. The city had that in its young architects, but it had to be matched by the talent of the developers' architects.

I was introduced to David Specter by Steve Quick, one of these able city architects. My role was to be a sort of chaperone to a negotiation going on between the city and a developer who had commissioned Specter to design a large building on East Fifty-seventh Street, in the middle of Manhattan. The developer signified a willingness to incorporate public amenities, including a public walkway through the building, in exchange for certain incentives designed to result in greater profit for him. Without going into detail, I might say that this was a negotiation to inspire some optimism in a city planning commissioner even in February or August.

So when the civic spirit is willing, and there is enough talent among the bureaucracy, there may yet be some hope for the pedestrian, with businesslike solutions to this urban problem. It is certainly not the largest problem of the cities, but it is pleasant to see some possibilities for improvement. Many a model can be found in this book, accumulated from the author's purposeful wanderings with a camera, but also needed are hard thinking, hard bargaining, and plenty of elbow time on a drafting board.

W. McQ.

1 INTRODUCTION

The concern of this book is cities, particularly modern cities, where the problems and the need for solutions are dramatized most clearly.

Will the exodus to suburbs, decentralization of industry, and deteriorating municipal services drain our cities of their vitality until they ultimately disappear, to be replaced by centerless sprawl and super-highways? I believe that we will always be attracted to cities or some future equivalent, in order to find what the state of nature does not provide: stimulus, contrast, excitement, economic reward, and the recognition of man's gregarious instincts. The quality of life in these cities will continue to interest the concerned citizen, whether or not he must live in them, and the designer, who will give them form. In this study of cities we shall focus on the pedestrian urban space, where the quality of life in a particular city may be most clearly perceived.

There is a qualitative difference among our personal experiences of urban spaces, and the essential characteristics present in successful ones—though often occurring accidentally—function in predictable and positive ways. It is useful for the architect or urban designer to add an analytic dimension to the layman's perception of cities, since the professional must learn first to identify and then to manipulate these tangible and intangible elements: the power of anticipation and surprise, the mystery of lighting, the pull of the waterfront, the excitement of arcades, the appeal of people-watching, the surfaces and objects of the city.

1

Whether the focus is the rehabilitation of an old inner-city core, the planning of a new metropolis in a wheat field, or a Soleri Arcology in outer space, there appear to be universals, whose appeal to urban man has transcended cultural and geographic barriers. Since an urban spatial experience which offered pleasure to a first-century Roman might still please a twenty-first-century citizen of the world, examining historical precedents is valid in shaping cities of today and tomorrow.

2

3

The move from country to city is as old as civilization itself. Aside from the obvious social and economic benefits, man is attracted by variety, for which he sacrifices serenity, and by excitement, for which he abandons his direct contact with nature.

4

5

6

7

8

Urban man tries to evoke that earlier closeness to natural phenomena: a fountain to suggest a natural watercourse; an urban park to simulate natural land-scape; a tower restaurant to recall the view from some long-forgotten mountaintop.

9

10

1

AN URBAN SPACE

12

Fotocielo, Rome

Our goal must be to provide pleasurable spaces for the activities a city encourages. Historically this requirement was assumed; today it is usually overlooked. We should seek to recreate not the specifics of earlier spaces, but the process and the human constants that generated them in their time.

Venice: unique but relevant, for it is a city where the pedestrian has always been supreme, where spaces are at his scale and accommodate his needs.

3

Fotocielo, Rome

Where only pedestrians may enter, people relax into natural activities, seek points of vantage, and form groups of common interest. Without the cacophonous threat of automobiles, the pace slows to a walk.

14

15

16

7

18

THE PLACE TO GO

19

The "place to go" is where people think the action is, and a sense of liveliness is the essence of the successful urban space. It may be very large or very small, monumental or intimate.

It may change its function from hour to hour; the successful urban space doesn't stand still to be photographed.

21

22

23

24

Like this town pump, it may have a specific use rein-
forcing, or in this case justifying, its social function.

Ancient Egyptians combined religious structures with spaces able to accommodate great numbers of people. Although the primary function of the space was to fulfill some collective religious ritual, it is probable that it functioned socially like an Italian piazza.

A kind of "hole" in the texture of a city, this is the place to watch and be watched, to participate or to avoid participation safely. It is a focus, a change of pace, a node or a point of emphasis or a breathing space, but always at the personal level of perception. Since it is for the pedestrian that the elements of successful urban spaces are manipulated, any meaningful discussion assumes his point of view.

27

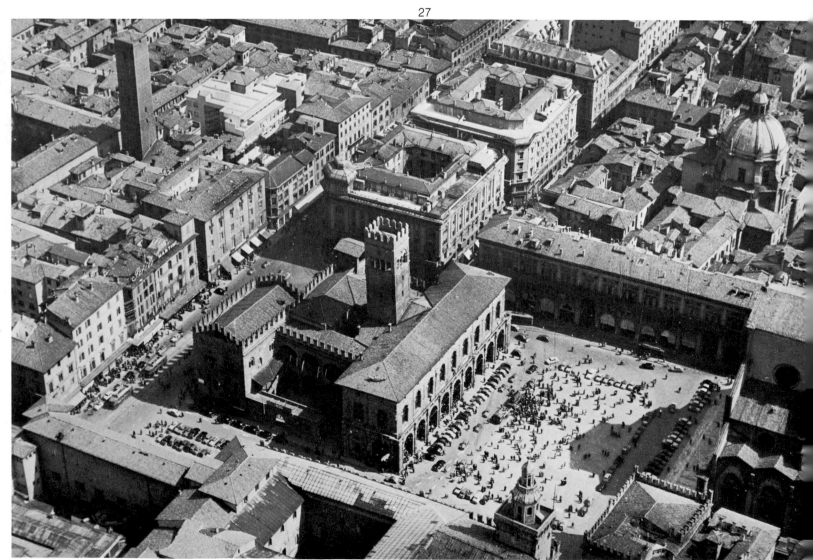

Fotocielo, Rome

28

29

THE FLOOR OF THE CITY
A PAVING
ANTHOLOGY

4

These two spaces have similar area and similar use. One is barren, uncrossable; the other somehow urban, live, human. The pattern of lines and geometric shapes and the changes of color as well as of texture provide a scale against which the pedestrian measures his movement. By visually breaking down large areas into more manageable bits, paving patterns help to "occupy" an area and render it more approachable.

31

Even shadows seem to create the necessary scale
underfoot—and if they seem to, they do.

These paving patterns are based on small, simple units. By combining these units, either with each other or with a limited number of other materials, designs of increasing complexity and decorative content are achieved.

34

35

36

37

38

39

40

41

A strong pattern can absorb minor visual interruptions. The sidewalk paving pattern used throughout downtown Copenhagen is scaled exactly to an average human stride. It has the effect of making one feel personally accommodated.

42

43

44

45

46

47

8

49

Imagine these areas (50, 52) without the pattern, and the visual function of the paving design becomes clear. One may conclude that the larger the space being treated, the more positive the pattern must be to achieve the desired sense of scale.

50

51

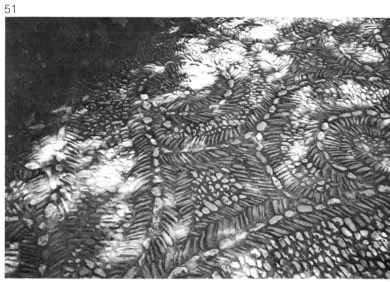

52

Paving can also supply information, both symbolically and literally. At night "Pettinelli Sport" is lit from beneath the sidewalk—a unique concept.

54

55

56

57

Barriers need not be walls or chains; this upended
brick pattern is just as effective.

An inducement to window-shop, subtle and mysteriously persuasive.

Here the symbolic and decorative are one, a unity
rarely achieved.

60

Sometimes lowly functions—in this case, storm drains—generate a decorative pattern.

Paved surfaces warped for drainage are camouflaged here by the linear pattern, so that at pedestrian eye-level the disconcerting undulations are concealed.

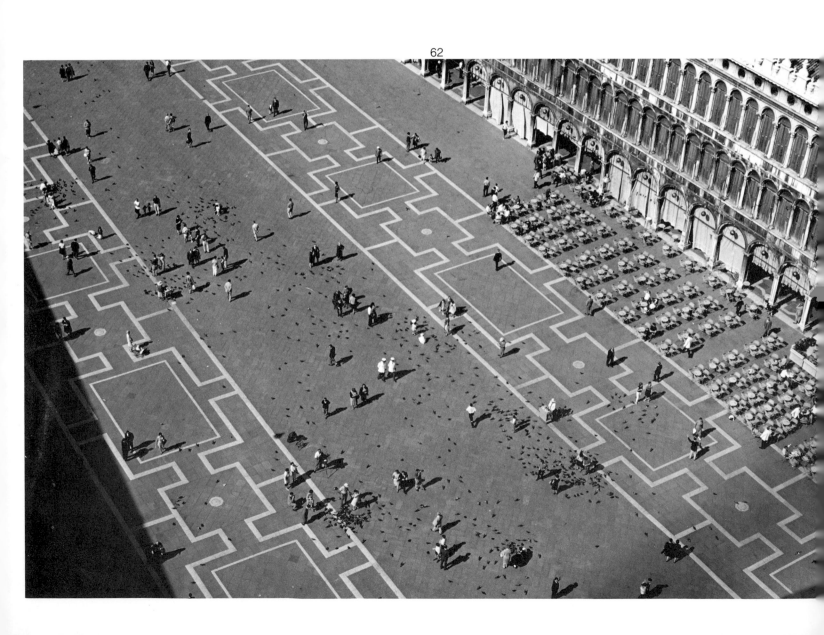

Within an overall geometric pattern such exquisite detail offers a point of focus, a visual pause, and yet another means of giving measure to motion.

This contemporary Manhattan example is an extraordinary combination of the practical and the decorative: while discouraging dogs, it allows rain and air to reach the tree roots.

66

A quietly inventive use for the urban floor: a precast trough to carry water across a sidewalk from roof leader to gutter.

67

Bicycle rack.

68

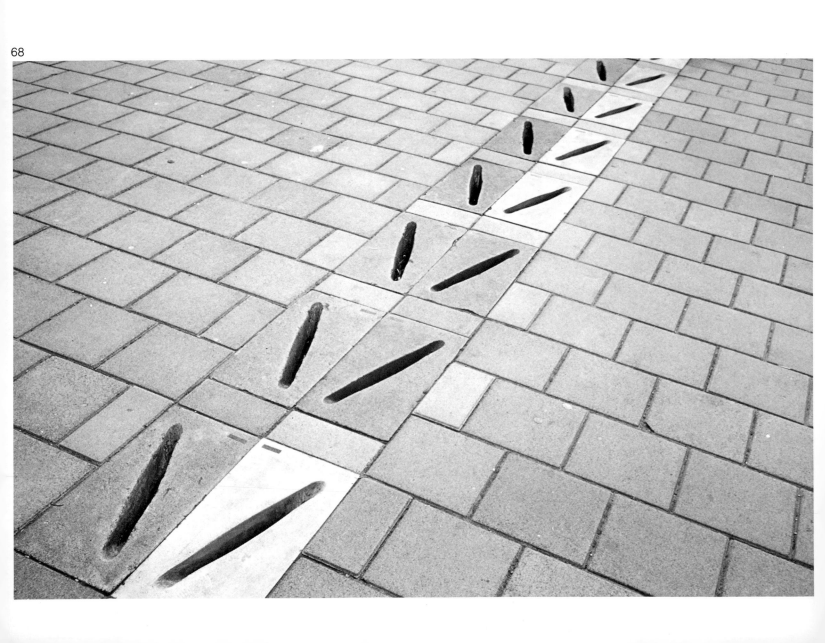

Sometimes—but not often—a bit of a city's paving fulfills and then transcends all of its functional, decorative and symbolic requirements. Better still if children discover they have a new toy, and best of all if the designer thought of it too.

69

70

Water. Mysterious, compelling. We have an atavistic need to participate in and with it. In its natural forms, it has enormous raw emotional content. Of all materials available to the designer, water comes closest to being a universal source of pleasure. Ada Louise Huxtable has written: "Its deeper implications suggest evanescent joys, cleansing of the spirit, the transience of perfection, the insubstantiality of dreams, the flowing continuity of life, and a consummate, fleeting beauty—impermanent, like all great romantic beauties, and therefore more beautiful than the tangible and real."[1]

71

Although an "unavailable" space in an urban set-
ting (72), large expanses of water redefine those parts
of the city which abut them. In other forms, water
invites participation.

72

73

". . . its pleasures are visual and auditory. . . . it is
a performance and a show. Its playful, changeable
range runs from the breathtakingly theatrical to
the mysteriously subtle. It is capable of broad jokes
and tenuous elegancies. Above all, it is an un-
paralleled instrument of grandeur and romance."[2]

75

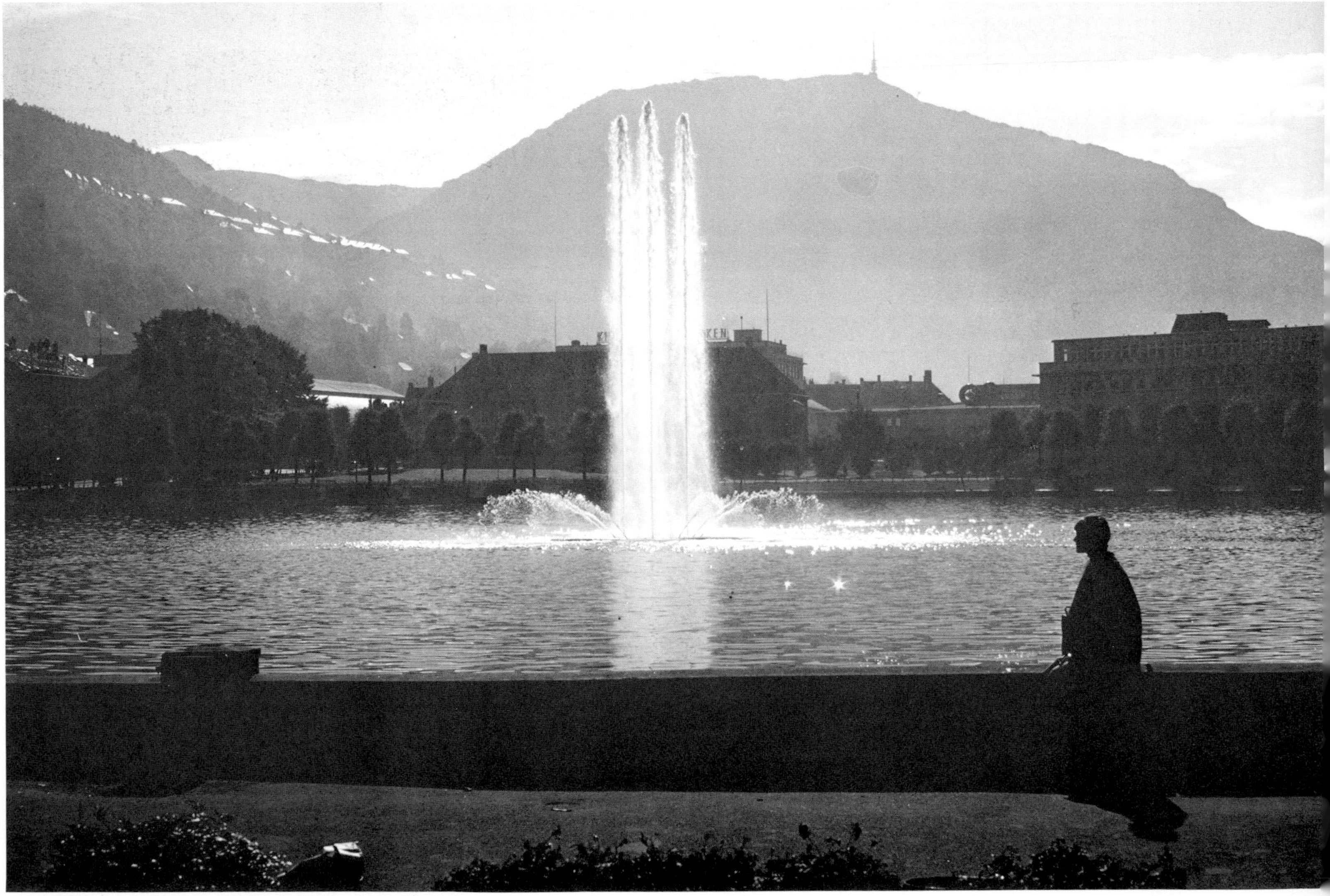

Unique among urban surfaces, water defines its own scale, constantly changing its color and texture in response to wind and sky. The sound and look of water as fountain or pool can create a mood, an oasis in the urban fabric that delights and enriches the soul.

76

77

In its controlled, designed urban manifestations, water can induce different emotions by reference to its various natural states. Hence, a flamboyant fountain recalls the waterfall; a water basin evokes the limpid mountain pool.

78

79

80

Urban water attracts pedestrian activity; the edge of
the pool offers a smooth channel for strollers to follow.

81

Though totally surrounded by exhaust fumes and raucous noise, this tiny fountain provides an alternate focus that dominates the surroundings.

82

83

Fire, rarely used as an urban amenity today, is the
implied source of the magic in these public fountain
displays (84).

84

Landscape architect Lawrence Halprin understands the need people feel to be involved with water, even vicariously (85, 86), and has created an implicitly theatrical, open-ended environment whose intent was ".... that as a result of the process of design (which was incomplete without people involved in the performance of the work) participation would result."

This vest-pocket park in mid-Manhattan (87) exploits the "white noise" of a waterfall to screen out traffic noise, and directs all visual attention away from the street.

85

86

87

Eugene Cook

WATERFRONT
THE CITY'S EDGE

Water is the best edge a city can have. It creates at the same time a barrier and a sense of unlimited space. It reflects by night and cools by day. Waterfront is any city's most valuable natural asset.

89

Zurich Tourist Office

Few cities exploit their natural waterfront sites as thoroughly as Zurich. The Limmat River flows through the city and empties into the Lake of Zurich, providing a variety of water-edge conditions, and a "how to" textbook on waterfront uses (89–94, 96).

90

91

92

93

Venice's Piazza San Marco is barely above sea level,
which results in a direct, unprotected relation to the
water (95, 97) and also creates a problem for the
future of the city.

94

95

96

97

Canals inevitably produce waterfront wherever they go. These New England barge canals (99) never were intended to be urban amenities, though that potential exists.

The bridges required to cross canals or rivers, by leading us up and over a body of water, give us a constantly changing perspective—hence, the visual richness of canal cities.

Without the reflections in the water, the reality is a garishly illuminated row of buildings. Urban designers must plan such visual "accidents."

7

103

104

105

106

107

LIGHTING

Lighting is sparkle, glow, jewelry, luminosity, magic, ambience, mystery, and much more. A practical level of urban lighting need not be accomplished by floodlighting; how much more festive to use many small low-output sources, not only for illumination but for guidance and graphics as well.

Where fixtures are chosen as the source of light, daytime and nighttime appearance must be considered equally. Appropriateness to the environment must govern the design.

108

110

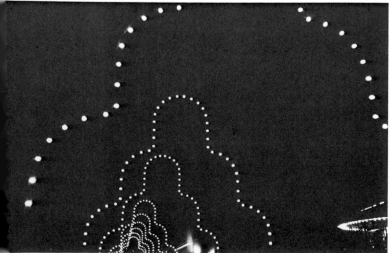

109

Repetition of a single component is the key to the successful design of many lighting fixtures, and—not irrelevantly—of much jewelry as well.

111

112

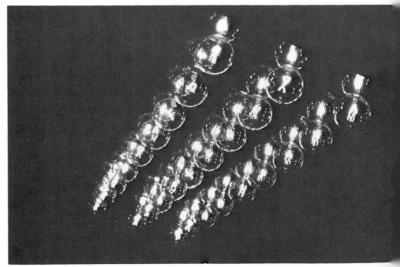

113

114

115

Some cities use a simple form as a common basis for widely-differing fixtures, as Stockholm and its satellite cities do with this spherical globe (116).

Backlighting is poetic, but need not be accidental. Ideally, the designer controls the placement of the elements of an urban space (117, 118).

116

117

118

Besides being minor foci of pedestrian activity, news-
stands, ordinary by day (120), provide at night (121)
an unexpected warmth, a welcome haven in the dark
city.

119

120

21

8

ANTICIPATION AND SURPRISE

Anticipation . . . of something, and of nothing. These
two photographs are abstracts of visual phenomena
that draw us through space, arousing our curiosity
and producing an intuitive sense of the imminence of
a different experience. . . .

23

124

125

126

Jean-Paul Sartre observed that the American street
is "a straight line that gives itself away immediately. It
contains no mystery." Observe the strange power of a
stairway to the unknown, the fascination of boxes
within boxes within boxes, a glimpse of spaces be-
yond, as yet unseen . . . and the peculiar perception
of two infinities at once (129).

Why are we drawn to the edge (130, 132)? Curiosity? Fear? Hope? Or perhaps our subconscious awareness that the normally high level of urban stimuli will be dramatically reduced when we reach that edge.

130

131

We sense that something *will* happen at the widening of the street (128). In the curving medieval street (131) and Boston arcades (133, 134), it *is* happening, a continuous visual revelation.

32

33

134

A vital skill of the urban designer is the ability to create visual suspense. By planning a vista or an orchestrated hierarchy of spaces, he will cause us consciously or unconsciously to experience surprise or excitement again and again, however familiar the sequence may become.

135

136

139

37

138

The rectilinear grid plan of many American cities makes the creation of such calculated vistas difficult. Given an irregular downtown layout, the Boston Redevelopment Authority carefully shaped spatial sequences with new and old structures, passing the monumental new City Hall, and coming to rest—visually—on historic Faneuil Hall.
Restoring older parts of a city or focusing attention on fine older buildings is not merely an intellectual exercise. The carefully preserved medieval inner cores of Stockholm and Zurich, and Boston's Back Bay area, offer the illusion of escape in time from the urban present, much as the height of San Francisco's Telegraph Hill or the Empire State Building offers a physical escape.

146

147

148

Rome's Spanish Steps—the world's most elaborate continuous bench—not only provide places for performers, audience, and catnappers, but also brilliantly connect two levels of the city.
The stairway (151) leading down to Central Park's Bethesda Fountain functions similarly.

149

150

151

Though set in the middle of Central Park, Bethesda Fountain draws weekend crowds from all over the city to watch the "show," and must qualify as an urban space through the sheer intensity and vitality of its use. Also significant is the particularly effective form of urban anonymity offered by the convex seating edge of the fountain basin. Conversely, intimacy would be encouraged by seating designs with opposite curvature. Straight-line benches are essentially neutral, maintaining anonymity by discouraging eye-to-eye contact.

152

People will sit on anything to become members of the urban audience, so the seats or steps or building foundation or flower urn might as well be the correct height for it.

153

154

The two-by-two design for this sea wall exhibits an extraordinary degree of human understanding and design sophistication. It represents a standard against which the design of much other "street furniture" might well be judged. Ada Louise Huxtable has written that such designs should not be "the self-conscious declaration of the designer, advertising his ingenuity and originality to the world. Nothing is in poorer taste than the strident insistence on the designer as an individual, for a captive audience in a public place . . . . the best street furniture is most remarkable for its unobtrusiveness . . . . for unobtrusiveness does not mean dullness. It is a subtle blend of suitability to purpose, harmony with locale, and low-key, but definite, visual pleasure."[3]

155

156

157

158

159

10

STREET FURNITURE

160

161

Paul Ryan

162

Under this general heading are grouped other objects that should quietly serve the urban space in some way—perhaps even with wit and humor: trash receptacles, clocks, drinking fountains, barriers, telephone booths, and kiosks.

163

Forsman Andersson

164

A spiked fence (165) clearly conveys its function as a barrier. Other more subtle solutions accomplish much the same result. The steep grassy slope (166) and the cobbled berm (169) are as effective and much more pleasant than a railing would be.

165

166

167

168

169

These concrete bollards (170) rimming the waterfront of a new American vacation community deftly incorporate lighting which will recreate this visual barrier at night. The stations of Mexico City's new subway system are identified by illuminated standards (171) incorporating symbolic representation of both the entire system and the particular station.

170

171

Robin Bath

Undistinguished by day, at night this telephone booth
(172) suggests the same sense of "haven" provided
by the illuminated kiosk (173).

172

173

Using display cases to extend the selling area of a shop is a technique frequently used in the enclosed malls of American regional shopping centers.

174

175

Few newsdealers are as imaginative as this one (176); simple repetition—as in some lighting design—gives visual order to what is characteristically a chaotic display. Fruit and flower vendors (177, 178) are small-scale, movable elements that can add vitality and artless charm to an urban space.

176

177

178

11

SURFACE ENRICHMENT

179

180

181

182

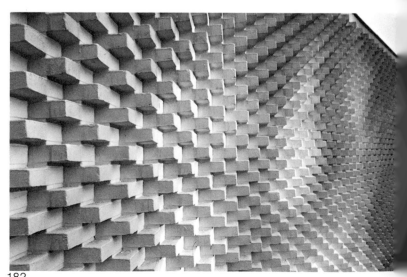

The spaces through which we move are shaped by real and implied surfaces. We walk between, on, and under them. They enclose buildings, guide us, and carry away the rain. As decoration, information, and another means to create a human scale, we respond to surface enrichment.

183

185

From the cave walls at Lascaux and Italian Renaissance church facades, to contemporary architects' efforts to make decorative use of structural and mechanical systems, man has expressed a need to embellish the surfaces around him. In an urban environment, such decorative detail offers continuing delight to the eye of the pedestrian.

186

187

189

190

Urban graphics guide and inform the public. In contrast to street furniture, which should be unobtrusive, graphics must be highly visible to serve their function.

188

191

A simple message may be reduced to a symbol (193, 194), be directed at a specific audience (192, 197, 200), or attract attention by extraordinary scale (195, 196, 199). More detailed announcements should always be as harmonious a part of the total scene as this street banner (198) or wall plaque (212).

192

193

194

195

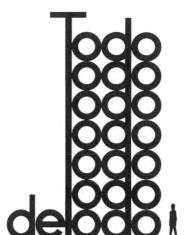

196

197

198

99

200

201

202

203

204

205

Although traffic-directing signs are usually permanent, advertising and announcement posters, which are temporary, are a much greater component of urban graphics, and contribute a strong element of change. The design and repetitive arrangement of these posters can produce chaos, charm, or boredom.

207

209

208

Graphics acquire even greater visual importance at night, when they may also serve as a light source (207, 209, 211). Recognizing that the conventional method of mounting neon letters on a solid vertical board would have visually destroyed the narrow street (208, 210), the designers made the letters practically transparent by day, with no loss of nighttime impact.

210

211

212

In this characteristically northern European approach to neon advertising, the letters are compatible with the building's architecture, and are essentially invisible in daylight. As the building disappears in darkness, the illuminated message appears, helping to "populate" the adjoining urban space (213, 214).

Signs painted directly on wooden boards are in the earliest American tradition. This example (215) is clear, direct, and sophisticated in spite of its simplicity.
If all other means are unavailing, we can populate our urban spaces this way (216)

213

214

215

216

SHELTERS

Unobtrusiveness once again is the criterion of successful design, in this case of shelters. These serve their purpose with style, yet remain subordinate to the activity they shelter.

The steel columns supporting the canvas roof (218) echo the lacing above, cast a similar shadow, and are actually less obtrusive in their complex design than a simpler solid column would have been.

217

218

CAFÉS

Sidewalk cafés provide a graceful transition between participation and non-involvement in the urban space, and between watching and being watched. They offer both privacy and exposure.

220

This French café represents the most common variety (220), located in or next to a building, with pedestrians walking between café and street. Another style (221) is even pleasanter: This Roman café turns its back to the street. The canopy is essential as a substitute for the psychological protection the building furnishes to the French café-sitters. Surrounded by pedestrian traffic, this Venetian café (222) is much more exposed, and must offer umbrellas, trees, or other implied protection overhead to attract sitters. Whether a café faces towards or away from or is surrounded by traffic, this sense of protection must exist.

221

222

The "street" may become a waterway (223, 224), the traffic, canal barges. The café may be just above the street (225) or—as a part of New York's new Fifth Avenue zoning—eighty-five feet up, overlooking the avenue (227).

223

224

225

226

227

15

228

VARIABLE PARTICIPATION

The ideal vantage point, protected above and behind, is an abstraction fulfilling a need for security probably of primeval origin. The tree-shaded bench (229) provides such a location. An arcade (228) is the spatial abstraction which provides these advantages: the observer is secure, psychologically invisible, able to observe the activity before him, and has the all-important option of participating or remaining on the sidelines.

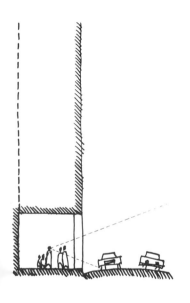

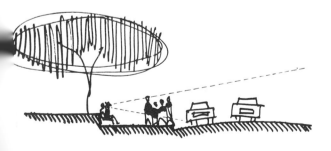

This pedestrian thoroughfare (230) excludes vehicular traffic, and shows an apparent intensification of activity: a sense of something happening. Though "air rights" schemes seem contemporary, arcades are ancient, and in some medieval Swiss cities, they were built by private purchasers of such rights over a public thoroughfare.

229

230

COVERED PEDESTRIAN STREETS

231

232

233

Milan's Galleria (231, 232, 234) is simply the intersection of two pedestrian streets. That it is roofed contributes to its popularity less than does the fact that it interconnects two major generators of pedestrian traffic. The dominantly vertical proportion of the space seems to intensify activity while creating a psychologically desirable sense of enclosure.

The main pedestrian route through Manhattan's proposed Battery Park City is also a "vertical" space and suggests the same quality of great activity. In contrast, the pedestrian street of a typical American shopping center (233) is often horizontal and "exposed" and by its width implies the presence of vehicular traffic, though none may exist.

234

235

MULTIPLE GENERATORS OF ACTIVITY

However clever the design, however rich the visual content, an urban space will never come to life unless people have multiple reasons for being there. Obviously, shopping facilities will generate activity. Rail, bus, and airline terminals bring predictable numbers of pedestrians into predictable parts of the city. High-density housing in close proximity to an urban space will encourage round-the-clock use of that space.

Apartments located directly over shops are common in older parts of cities, supplementing nighttime activity. Zoning, rather than forcing the segregation of these functions, should encourage their combination.

In a Swedish New Town (237) the shopping, transportation, and housing are clearly combined in a nearly diagrammatic manner. In the Battery Park City proposal (238) the waterfront adds yet another source of activity.

The problem of maintaining a desirable sense of daytime liveliness during evening "downtime" is uniquely handled in the heart of Copenhagen. By day, heavy pedestrian traffic moves from a transportation hub at Kongens Nytorv (A) and along the winding, completely pedestrian main shopping street (B). Passing through an even larger transportation interchange at the Town Hall Square (C), the route becomes a grand boulevard, passing Tivoli Amusement Park (D) and ending—diagrammatically speaking—at the main railroad station (E).

During the day, this linear urban space extends from A to E, populated from downtown Copenhagen's business district. At night, with only a fraction of the daytime population, the city responds—in a sense—by shortening this linear route. Kongens Nytorv goes to sleep, the main shopping thoroughfare shifts to window-shopping and scattered night life, and the real activity is concentrated in a relatively short stretch between the Town Hall Square and the main railroad station, with substantial input from increased nighttime activity at Tivoli. The result is "a place to go" both day and night. In short, an urban space.

236

Aerodan Luftfoto

237

238

239

240

241

242

THE SHOPPING STREET

Another kind of diagram is represented by Zurich's Bahnhofstrasse. This main shopping street runs from the railroad station—a dynamic urban space itself (239)—to a park commanding spectacular views of lake and mountains (242). The street is relatively narrow (241), and traffic is not heavy enough to create a serious obstacle to "cross-shopping." Parallel and close by, waterfront promenades on the Limmat River offer visual relief and an alternate route at any point. The cross section suggests a basilica, with low-ceilinged "aisles" and a "nave" of infinite height, created by the low canopy of trees over the sidewalks and the sky between. The shopper is given a sense of being in an arcade, when in fact he is not. Barcelona's Ramblas is similar, with an office-commercial-transportation center at one end and the waterfront at the other (244). It is carved out of a dense medieval part of the city, offering intricate ways on and off this broad pedestrian thoroughfare. Since vehicular traffic separates the main walkway from the shops, the Ramblas is not as successful a shopping street as it is a remarkable social center (243, 245).

243

245

244

Trabajos Aereos y Fotogrametricos

19

246

247

248

A HIERARCHY OF PEDESTRIAN SPACES

Venice is unique and unduplicable. It is also highly relevant to this study of pedestrian spaces, since the streets of Venice have been shaped and sized only in response to human—not to vehicular—needs. Most cities imply the presence of wheeled vehicles of some sort in the widths of their streets or the curve of a sidewalk, so that even in pedestrian precincts the vehicle is "present."

Venice would be a significant model for this reason alone, but it also effectively separates pedestrian from vehicular—albeit waterborne—traffic. As a canal city it offers the pedestrian visual richness as a result of his constantly changing eye level. And because all of its streets and spaces are pedestrian and sharply defined, we can see and experience what kind or size of street will properly contain which human activities: a hierarchy of pedestrian spaces. We can learn how wide a main pedestrian shopping street really needs to be (248, 249), or how narrow (247) a side street may become, so that a shopper can see into show windows on both sides of the street at the same time.

We may conclude that variations in width, perhaps
from as narrow as eleven or twelve feet, and occasion-
al irregular broadenings into usable "piazzettas,"
are far more interesting and dynamic than a constant
width. We will probably be made aware of just which
familiar elements of our cities have been shaped
by vehicles. We will experience in Venice a strongly
vertical cross section in most of the spaces, determined by the necessity of building high where "land"
is at a premium. Though they are open to the sky,
we experience in these spaces a pleasant and satis-
fying sense of enclosure, which increases after dark.
Inextricably linked with this variety in horizontal dimension, we find that the myriad canals and bridges add
seemingly infinite variety in three-dimensional space.

250

251

This project for midtown Manhattan (251) incorporates the relative narrowness, vertical proportion, and infinite height of a Venetian street into a daylit, air-conditioned shopping concourse below street level. Pedestrian activity would be insured by direct connections to the subway system at this level, and to the lobby of an office building directly above.

252

253

254

255

256

The hierarchy of pedestrian spaces encompasses a broad range of sizes and shapes. The smallest are no more than street widenings sufficient to accommodate a quiet conversation. Larger spaces (255) may relate to a bridge or a church, and find room for a restaurant in a corner. The hierarchy is completed by a public outdoor space culminating in a spectacular view of the lagoon (257). This is the living room of Venice, the *spazio per dolce far niente*—"space for beautiful doing nothing."

257

20

DIRECTIONS
A:WATERFRONT USE

261

The shop-lined harbor of Portofino (261) draws its charm from the intimate relationship between water and pedestrian. This café (262) in Manhattan's new "Waterside" housing community overlooking the busy East River suggests the same quality in a different context.

259

Port of New York Authority

Municipal planning agencies throughout the United States have begun to acknowledge that their function must not be limited to proscriptive zoning, but be broadened to deal positively with the subjective quality of urban environment. The administrative methods and specific development potential of each city, of course, vary, but there appear to be certain common areas of concern. Although New York is hardly typical of American cities, and Manhattan Island still less so, certain problems and their rather innovative solutions can be taken as representative of a developing pattern throughout the country. Manhattan Island (258) has perhaps the world's longest waterfront in direct contact with high density urban areas. It shocks visitors to learn that this marvelous natural amenity is accessible to the public at very few points, usually in direct competition with peripheral highway traffic. This schematic proposal for the southern tip of Manhattan (259, 260) suggests small harbors created by building out into the water and surrounded by activity-producing housing and office space. Since the area now occupied by obsolete finger piers is under municipal rather than private control, private developers wishing to participate must follow guidelines established by city planning agencies. They can, for example, be required to incorporate into their projects waterfront pedestrian promenades, specified commercial areas, parks, or rights-of-way for small-scale public transportation.

260

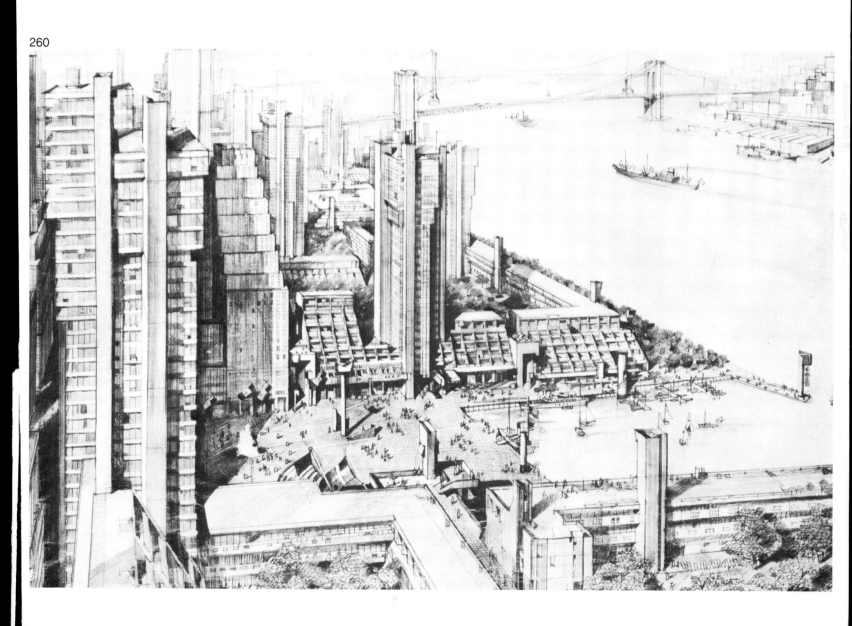

Separately, arcades and waterfronts attract and intrigue us. Their combination, as in Zurich's Limmat River promenade (263), is uniquely potent. As proposed by New York State's Urban Development Corporation, Welfare Island in the East River would be developed as a totally pedestrian environment. One main public space combines housing, shops, and a transportation terminal (264).

The Graphic Arts Center (266), a highly innovative housing complex proposed for Manhattan's lower west side, must reach over the peripheral highway to make contact with the water. The most farsighted of several proposals for the rebuilding of this highway would relocate it at the western outer ends of the obsolete finger piers which exist almost uninterruptedly from the Battery to 72nd street. Over the new highway and the area now occupied by the piers, a deck would support housing, commercial space, and parks, all in direct contact with the river's edge.

263

264

DIRECTIONS B: INCENTIVE ZONING

Zoning is the single most potent force shaping our cities. A clear trend is developing to use it as a positive force in urban planning instead of as a merely proscriptive process. Developers are offered financially irresistible bonuses in the form of extra buildable floor area in exchange for specified amenities. Designs incorporating new legitimate theaters (265) command such bonuses in an area of Manhattan designated the "Special Theater District," so that this process should help to replace aging theaters with new ones and encourage the future of legitimate theater in New York City.

The trend towards creating large "special districts," within which zoning is aimed at a coordinated result, is replacing the method of considering building lots as isolated entities. The Special Fifth Avenue District is intended to preserve the avenue as an elegant shopping street by *requiring* retail space at ground level, encouraging pedestrian arcades parallel to the avenue, and simultaneously mandating a specified and coordinated architectural form (267).

Still another type of special district is exemplified by one in Lower Manhattan that will—using the bonus system—give the developer options to provide various above-street bridges, shopping arcades, loggias, and so on, whose locations in accordance with an overall master plan have been determined in advance.

In short, these ingenious methods harness the profit incentive in private development to serve the ends of rational urban space planning.

266
Ezra Stoller Associates Inc.

267

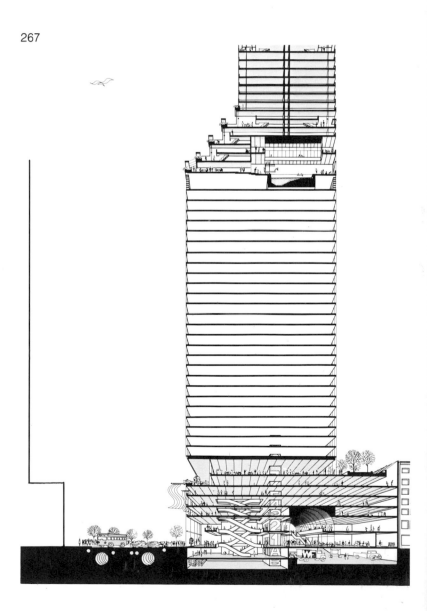

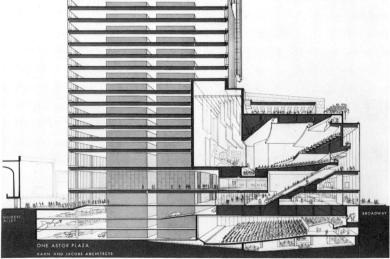

265

DIRECTIONS
C:PEDESTRIAN STREETS

268

Although the rectilinear grid pattern of many American cities implies that traffic is evenly distributed over the grid, this is not usually the case. Certain streets can be converted—either permanently or at specified hours—to pedestrian use without seriously impairing traffic flow. Minneapolis's Nicollet Mall (270, 271) replaced a conventional street with a relatively narrow winding roadway for bus service and pedestrian walks of varying width.

Manhattan's Madison Avenue has successfully experimented with the idea (268), and a permanent conversion is planned (269). After the initial novelty and excitement have worn off, the retail shops should continue to benefit from the quieter, cleaner, more relaxed atmosphere of a pedestrian street.

269

270

271

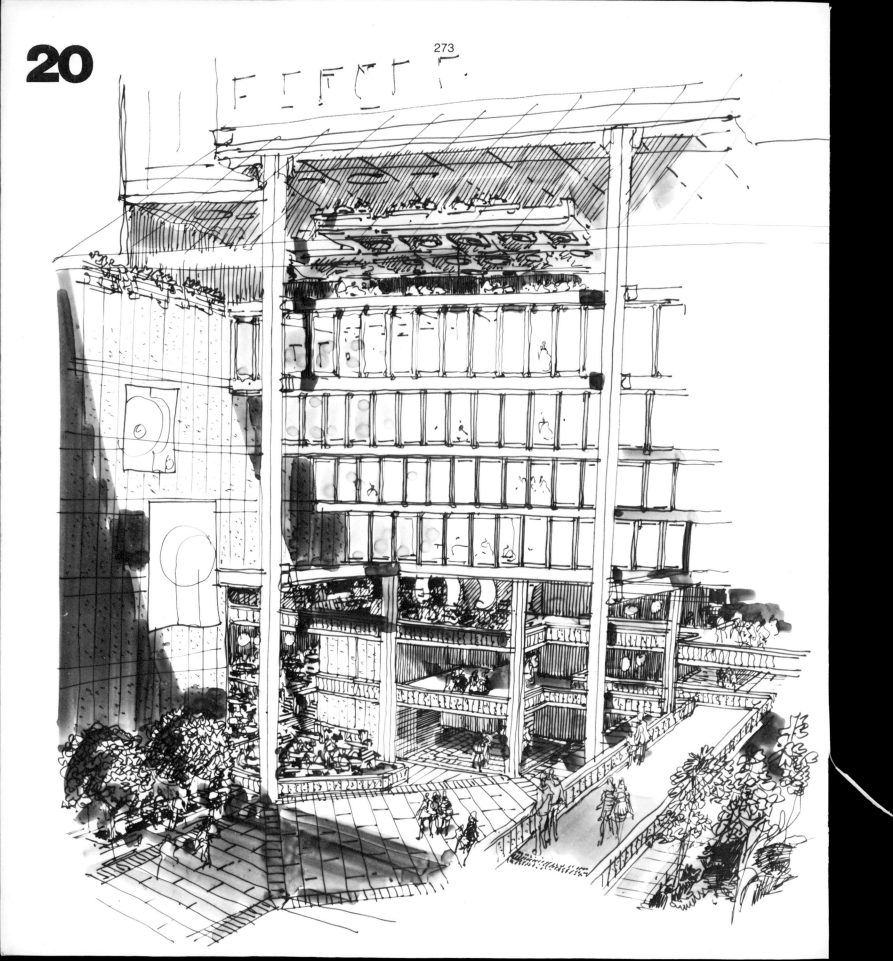

DIRECTION D: COVERED PEDESTRIAN SPACES

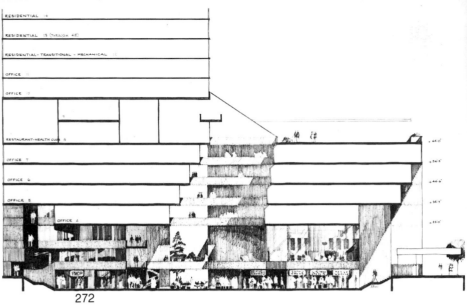

272

We tend to think of our units of city design in terms of the blocks rather than the public spaces we experience. The most significant new conception in New York City's zoning is that of the "Covered Pedestrian Space," for it extends public streets and avenues *into* the building itself. It is not an incidental connection between two streets. It is, in fact, defined in such a manner that it should become a dynamic urban space unto itself. The idea that urban spaces can be inside buildings should not be surprising to anyone who has been in Grand Central Station or the old Pennsylvania Station, and is probably most appropriate to northern climates. Though well-intended, zoning laws encouraging monumental outdoor plazas as settings for office towers simply do not create urban spaces. To quote from the New York City Zoning Resolution:

"A Covered Pedestrian Space is an enclosed area directly accessible to the public from an adjoining street, arcade, plaza . . . which is part of the public circulation system, and which has an area of at least 1500 square feet and a minimum width . . . of 20 feet . . . a height of at least 30 feet . . . has maximum feasible (retail) frontage. . . . In no event may banks, loan offices, insurance offices or similar office-type uses occupy any portion of the frontage. . . . is adequately illuminated, utilizing normal daylight wherever possible. . . . is kept open to the public between 7 a.m. and 12 midnight or on a schedule to meet the public need. . . . Planting, landscaping, ornamental fountains, statuary, bazaar furniture, kiosks, works of art, light wells . . . may be permitted. . . . A portion . . . shall be developed as public sitting areas with appropriate facilities such as cafés or other public seating. . . . entrances to lobbies may be permitted along the boundary of a Covered Pedestrian Space. . . . Where a lot is bounded by more than one street . . . the Covered Pedestrian Space will provide a connection. . . . For the purpose of insuring prominent public attention to the Covered Pedestrian Space, the openings at the face of the building . . . shall be at least 20 feet wide, 30 feet high . . . and unobstructed for a depth of 30 feet. . . ."

By means of the now familiar bonus system, the legislation encourages the creation of pedestrian spaces within buildings that interconnect adjoining streets. It requires retail shops and other attractions in these spaces to remain open most of the day. A building designed by the author (272, 273) which incorporates these features is scheduled for completion in 1974. It will connect 57th and 58th Streets just east of Park Avenue and contains a 100-foot-high skylit space with the potential of accommodating concerts and other cultural events.

It seems that new kinds of urban spaces will appear, suited to the climate and the temperament of our people, and made economically feasible by the ingenuity of our city planners. The successful urban space will be a dynamic and complex blend of the rational and the irrational, the planned and the un-intentional. Its universal constant will be its essential humanity, its accommodation of people's need to be at once individuals and part of their city.

274

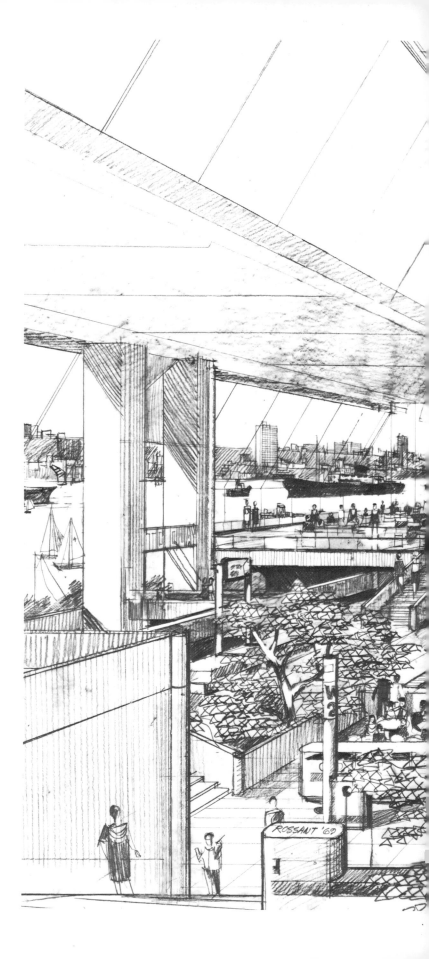

INDEX TO PHOTOGRAPHS

Photographs by the author except as noted.

NOTES

240. Zurich (photo: Zurich National Tourist Office).

243, 245. Barcelona.

244. Barcelona (photo: Trabajos Aereos y Fotograметricos).

246-250. Venice. (**249** photo: Fotocielo, Rome).

251. Project under consideration for midtown Manhattan site (design: David Kenneth Specter; rendering: L. Olin).

252-257. Venice.

258. New York, New York (photo: Port of New York Authority).

259, 260. New York, New York (architects: Conklin & Rossant; Wallace, McHarg, Roberts & Todd; rendering: James S. Rossant). Prepared for the Lower Manhattan Plan.

261. Portofino, Italy.

262. "Waterside" (design: Davis, Brody & Associates, Architects; rendering: Bergmann).

263. Zurich.

264. Town Harbor, Welfare Island, New York (design: Philip Johnson & John Burgee, Architects; rendering: Ronald Love).

265. One Astor Plaza, New York (design: Kahn & Jacobs, Architects).

266. Graphic Arts Center, New York (design: Paul Rudolph, Architect; photo: Ezra Stoller Associates Inc.).

267. Prototypical building section for Special Fifth Avenue District (design: Office of Midtown Planning and Development).

268. New York, New York.

269. Madison Avenue, New York (design: Van Ginkel Associates; rendering: B. Johnson).

270, 271. Minneapolis, Minnesota (design: L. Halprin; photo: Paul Ryan).

272. New York, New York (design: David Kenneth Specter, Architect; rendering: Gerald L. Jonas). Cross section through building.

273. *Op. cit.* Rendering of interior skylit space.

274. Battery Park City, New York (for credits see 235).

1. Ada Louise Huxtable, "Water: The Wine of Architecture," *Horizon,* May 1962, pp.10–16. Copyright © 1962 American Heritage Publishing Co., Inc.

2. Huxtable, *op. cit.*

3. Huxtable, "Street Furniture," *Horizon,* November 1959, pp.105–112. Copyright © 1959 Ada Louise Huxtable.